DAISY MILLER & TURN OF THE SCREW

NOTES

including
- *Introduction*
- *Life and Background*
- *List of Characters for each novel*
- *General Plot Summaries for each novel*
- *Summaries and Commentaries for each novel*
- *Critical Notes*
- *Questions for Review*
- *Selected Bibliography*

by
James L. Roberts, Ph.D.
Department of English
University of Nebraska

Cliffs Notes

INCORPORATED

LINCOLN, NEBRASKA 68501

Editor

Gary Carey, M.A.
University of Colorado

Consulting Editor

James L. Roberts, Ph.D.
Department of English
University of Nebraska

Cliffs Notes, Inc.   Lincoln, Nebraska

CONTENTS

Critical Essays

Questions for Review

Selected Bibliography

INTRODUCTION

AUTHOR'S LIFE AND BACKGROUND

Henry James was a true cosmopolite. He was a citizen of the world and moved freely in and out of drawing rooms in Europe, England, and America. He was perhaps more at home in Europe than he was in America, but the roots of his life belong to the American continent. Thus, with few exceptions, most of his works deal with some type of confrontation between an American and a European.

Henry James was born in New York in 1843. His father, Henry James, Sr., had inherited a considerable sum of money and spent his time in leisured pursuit of theology and philosophy. The father often wrote essays and treatises on aspects of religion and philosophy and developed a certain degree of mysticism. Among the guests in the James household were some of the most famous minds of the mid-nineteenth century. Henry James was able to hear his father converse with people like Ralph Waldo Emerson, Bronson Alcott, and George Ripley. The father was insistent that his children learn to approach life with the broadest possible outlook.

In the strictest sense of the word, Henry James had no formal education. As a youth, he had private tutors. Then in his twelfth year, his father took the entire family to Europe, where they moved freely from Switzerland to France to Germany in pursuit of stimulating conversation and intellectual ideas. The world of Europe left an everlasting impression on young Henry James. He was ultimately to return and make his home in Europe.

When the family returned from Europe, the elder James decided to settle in New England. He chose Cambridge because this was the center of American intellectual thought. Many of the writers of Cambridge, Boston, and nearby Concord, where Emerson and Thoreau lived, were often visitors in the James household. It was in Boston that James met the first great influence on his literary career. He established a close friendship with William Dean Howells, who as editor of one of America's leading magazines, was able to help James in his early efforts to write and publish.

In Boston, Henry James enrolled briefly in the Harvard Law School but soon withdrew to devote himself to writing. His older brother, William James, the most famous philosopher and psychologist America had yet produced, was also a student at Harvard, where he remained after graduation to become one of the most eminent lecturers in America.

By the late 1860's, James had done some reviewing and had sold one work of fiction to the *Atlantic Monthly*. He also went to Europe on his own, to see the continent as an adult. He returned again to Cambridge and New York in the hope of continuing his literary career, but he gradually came to the realization that Europe was more suitable for his writings. Thus, in 1876, when he was in his thirty-third year, James made the momentous decision to take up residence abroad. With the exception of short trips to various parts of the world, he lived the rest of his life in and near London. Until 1915, he retained his American citizenship, but when World War I broke out, he became a naturalized citizen of England in protest over America's failure to enter the war against Germany.

James' life and background were ideally suited for the development of his artistic temperament. Even though he was not extremely wealthy, he did have sufficient independent means to allow him to live a leisured life. His father's house provided all the intellectual stimulation he needed. The visitors were the most prominent artists of the day, and James was able to follow the latest literary trends. In his travels, he moved in the best society of two continents and came into contact with a large variety of ideas.

With such a life, it is natural that James' novels are concerned with a society of people who are interested in subtle ideas and subtle refinements. There are no really poor people in his novels. He wrote about people who had enough money to allow them to develop and cultivate their higher natures. His novels develop with a deliberate slowness and conscientious refinement. Many critics and readers resent the deliberate withholding of information and the slow development found in the Jamesian novel, but James' life was lived with a high degree of leisure and refinement. And finally, James was the first American qualified to develop the theme of the American in Europe. By the time he made his decision to settle in Europe, he had made several trips there and had lived and attended school in several parts of Europe. Thus, the subject matter of most of James' works is concerned with an American of some degree of innocence meeting or becoming involved with some European of experience.

In spite of his decision to live abroad, James remained essentially American in his sympathies. His greatest characters (or central characters) are almost always Americans. But at the same time, some of his most unpleasant characters are also Americans. But the important thing is that the characters who change, mature, and achieve an element of greatness are almost always Americans.

THE REALISM OF HENRY JAMES

Henry James has had a tremendous influence on the development of the novel. Part of this influence has been through the type of realism that he employs. On the other hand, the most frequent criticism against James has been that he is not realistic enough. Many critics have objected that James does not write about life, that his novels are filled with people whom one would never meet in this world. One critic (H. L. Mencken) suggested that James needed a good whiff of the Chicago stockyards so as to get a little life into his novels. Others have suggested that James' world is too narrow and incomplete to warrant classification as a realistic depiction of life.

Actually James' realism is of a special sort. By the early definitions, James is not a realist. The early definitions stated that the novelist should accurately depict life and that the novel should "hold up a mirror to life"; in other words, the realist was supposed to make an almost scientific record of life.

But James was not concerned with all aspects of life. There is nothing of the ugly, the vulgar, the common, or the pornographic in

James. He was not concerned with poverty or with the middle class who had to struggle for a living. Instead, he was interested in depicting a class of people who could afford to devote themselves to the refinements of life.

What then is James' special brand of realism? When we refer to James' realism, we mean James' fidelity to his own material. To best appreciate his novels and his realism, we must enter into James' special world. It is as though we ascended a ladder and arrived at another world. Once we have arrived at this special world and once we accept it, then we see that James is very realistic. That is, in terms of his world, he never violates his character's essential nature. Thus, James' realism, in the truest sense, means being faithful to his character. In other words, characters from other novels often do things or commit acts that don't seem to blend in with their essential nature. But the acts of the Jamesian character are always understandable in terms of that character's true nature.

James explained his own realism in terms of its opposition to romanticism. For James the realistic represents those things which, sooner or later, in one way or another, everyone will encounter. But the romantic stands for those things which, with all the efforts and all the wealth and facilities of the world, we can never know directly. Thus, it is conceivable that one can experience the same things that the characters are experiencing in a James novel: but one can never actually encounter the events narrated in the romantic novel.

When James, therefore, creates a certain type of character early in the novel, this character will act in a consistent manner throughout the entire book. This is being realistic. The character will never do anything that is not logical and acceptable to his realistic nature, or to our conception of what that character should do.

Writing about realism in later years, James maintained that he was more interested in a faithful rendition of a character in any given situation than in depicting all aspects of life. Accordingly, when he has once drawn Winterborne's or Daisy Miller's character in one situation, the reader can anticipate how that person will act in any other given situation. Likewise, the governess' actions, even in view of possible unrealistic apparitions, are always consistent. We are always able logically to understand all the actions of any character. Thus James' realism would never allow the characters to perform actions which would be inconsistent with their true natures.

STRUCTURE

Almost all of James' novels are structured in the same way. There must be a center — something toward which all the lines point and which "supremely matters." This is essentially James' own explanation of his structure. The thing that "supremely matters" is the central idea of the novel or that idea around which the novel functions. In *Daisy Miller,* the thing that "supremely matters" is Winterborne's attempt to discover how innocent Daisy really is. That is, could she possibly be a mistress of the art of deception and in truth be essentially an improper girl, or is she simply responding so innocently and spontaneously to life that she ignores all the rules of decorum. Thus, every scene is structured to illustrate something more about Daisy's personality. Likewise, in *The Turn of the Screw,* the thing that "supremely matters" is the innocence of the young children. Consequently, every scene and every action is designed to further illuminate this question. We are constantly pondering the relative innocence or evil of the young children.

James' creative process is also important to understanding the structure of his works. He begins his novels with a situation and a character. Many writers — like Nathaniel Hawthorne — would begin with an idea or theme in mind and then would create a situation and characters to illuminate the basic idea, but James' technique is just the opposite. He created a certain situation, and then he would place his characters in it. James would then, in effect, sit back and simply observe what would happen when a character was confronted with this new situation. Often, James said, he had no particular ending in mind when he began a novel. Instead, he would let the character and situation determine the outcome. This allowed him more freedom and allowed him the opportunity of "getting to know" his character by observing him in a series of scenes.

Thus, the central situation in *Daisy Miller* is the arrival in Europe of a charming young girl who feels restricted by the formalized rules of behavior in Europe. Owing to her failure to observe certain social restrictions, she is considered improper by many people. But others recognize that her actions are a part of her free American ways and maintain that she is innocent. Consequently, Daisy is placed in various situations where we can observe her actions and determine to what degree she is innocent and spontaneous.

The central situation in *The Turn of the Screw* involves the governess' view of her charges. Consequently, certain situations are created so that we may watch the governess react to the innocence or evil of her pupils.

We have said that all lines must point toward the thing that supremely matters, but these lines do not follow a straight course. This is not the way James structures his novels. Everything in the novel is aimed at the central situation, but he moves toward the center by exploring all the related matters. In other words, the structure could be best described by a series of circles around the center. Each circle is an event which illuminates the center, but highlights only a part of it. Each circle then is often a discussion by several different people. For example, one character observes something and then goes to another person to discuss his observation. Then two other characters might discuss the same event. By the end of the various discussions, James has investigated all of the psychological implications inherent in this particular situation. This would represent one circle. Then, we go to another event or situation, which will be fully discussed before proceeding to the next. Thus by the end of the novel, James has probed and examined every moral, ethical, and psychological aspect of the central situation, and the reader has heard the views of many people on the same subject.

Consequently, the structure of James' novels are circular in approach to the central subject, but every circle in some way illuminates the thing that supremely matters. Every incident functions to tell us more about a character or situation. There is nothing that is superfluous or extraneous.

DAISY MILLER

LIST OF CHARACTERS

Daisy Miller
A young, exceptionally pretty, young lady from the United States who shocks the more formalized European society by her spontaneous acts.

Mrs. Miller
Daisy's mother, who seems to sanction most of Daisy's erratic actions.

Winterborne
The narrator of the story and an acquaintance of Daisy Miller.

Mrs. Costello
Winterborne's aunt, who acts as his confidante; she thoroughly disapproves of Daisy Miller.

Mrs. Walker
A mutual friend of both Winterborne and Daisy Miller who later severs her relationship with Daisy.

Mr. Giovanelli
A handsome young Italian whom Daisy picks up in Rome.

GENERAL PLOT SUMMARY

In a Swiss resort, Winterborne meets a pretty young American girl who seems to have no qualms about talking to strangers. During the course of their conversation, she mentions her desire to visit the castle across the lake. Winterborne declares that he would be delighted to accompany her.

A few days later, Daisy introduces him to her mother, and Winterborne fears that Mrs. Miller will deeply disapprove of his invitation. Instead, Mrs. Miller readily agrees as long as she does not have to go along. That night Daisy suggests a boat ride on the lake. Even though it would be improper, Daisy insists, but she suddenly changes her mind on learning that her brother is in bed. Winterborne is perplexed and confused by her actions.

Winterborne is aware that it was highly indiscreet for Daisy to go with him to the castle, but he is so charmed and pleased by her spontaneity and gaiety that he is willing to overlook everything else. Furthermore, he is convinced she was acting with perfect innocence.

Winterborne wants to introduce Daisy to his aunt, a Mrs. Costello, but this elderly lady has heard enough about the young American girl to think her common and vulgar, and consequently, refuses to meet her.

During the visit to the castle, Daisy learns that Winterborne has to leave the next day. After teasing him about being under the influence of some woman, she makes him promise to visit her in Rome that winter.

Some months later, Winterborne does go to Rome and immediately hears that Miss Daisy Miller is being "talked about." She is accused of picking up strange men and being seen with them in indiscreet places. At the house of a mutual friend, Mrs. Walker, Daisy meets and teases Winterborne again. Soon she mentions that she is going for a walk in order to meet a Mr. Giovanelli. Mrs. Walker is shocked and tries to tell Daisy how improper it would be to be seen walking the streets. Daisy solves this by asking Winterborne to accompany her.

After Daisy meets her companion, the three of them stroll about for a while. In a few minutes, Mrs. Walker drives up in her carriage and tries to convince Daisy to come with her. She lets the girl know how improper it is to be seen walking along the street with a man. Daisy thinks that if what she is doing is improper, then she is completely improper and asks the others to forget about her.

Later, at a party given by Mrs. Walker, Daisy offends her hostess by coming very late with her Italian friend. When Daisy leaves,

Mrs. Walker snubs her and later tells Winterborne that Daisy will never again be allowed at her home.

For some time, Winterborne hears additional stories about Daisy, but he still maintains that she is an innocent but impetuous girl. He even tries to warn her about her indiscretions, but she is unconcerned. Winterborne continues to believe in Daisy's innocence until he passes by the Colosseum late one night. He enters to observe the arena and accidentally sees Daisy with her Italian friend. Then he realizes that she is not a young lady that a gentleman need be respectful to.

Winterborne advises Daisy to leave immediately, and he questions the Italian's intentions in bringing her there so late. A few days after this, Daisy catches the Roman fever, which causes her death. Three times during a period of consciousness, Daisy sent Winterborne a message which he could only interpret at a later date. He realized that Daisy was a very innocent girl who would have welcomed someone's esteem.

Note to the reader: Henry James revised almost all of his work for a final edition. Therefore, sometimes *Daisy Miller* appears with four sections, as is found in the following analysis. But it is just as possible to find it divided in only two sections. In this division, Section I combines the first two sections, that is, the episodes which take place in Switzerland, and Section II handles the Italian episodes.

SUMMARIES AND COMMENTARIES

SECTION 1

Summary

In the town of Vevey, Switzerland, a young gentleman named Winterborne has stopped to visit his aunt. But because she is "now shut up in her room smelling camphor," he has a large amount of free time. The town of Vevey is, in the summer time, so filled with Americans that one could almost consider it an American resort.

Winterborne usually spends most of his time in Geneva, where it is rumored that he is studying, but in the summer he always pays this visit to his aunt.

While Winterborne is sitting in a cafe drinking a cup of coffee, a child about nine or ten comes up to him and asks for a lump of sugar. Winterborne grants the request but admonishes the boy that sugar is not good for the teeth. The boy responds that he has virtually no teeth anyway. The boy is an American and maintains that the trouble with his teeth results from the dreadful European hotels and climate. What he really misses is some good American candy. Everything that is American seems better to the boy than anything European.

While Winterborne is talking with the young boy, they notice a pretty girl approach. The boy announces that it is his sister and Winterborne observes that American girls are indeed pretty. The young lady approaches and begins to reprimand young Randolph for various things. As she talks with her brother, Winterborne observes that she is a very charming creature who seems to have a lot of confidence in life.

He offers a passing remark to her and then wonders if he has been too forward. In Geneva, "a young man wasn't at liberty to speak to a young unmarried lady save under certain rarely-occurring conditions." But Winterborne tries to make another remark: he asks her if they are planning to go to Italy. After a few more remarks, he is able to determine that the young lady is "really not in the least embarrassed." In fact, she seems perfectly relaxed and composed.

After a brief conversation, Winterborne observes her more closely. She possesses remarkable and expressive features, but there is a "want of finish." Her conversation is quite pleasant, and she tells Winterborne that she comes from New York State. He addresses the young boy by asking for his name. The boy blurts out that he is Randolph C. Miller and wants to tell his sister's name. She tells him to be quiet until the man asks for it. Winterborne assures her that he would like to know her name. Randolph explains that his sister uses the name of Daisy Miller, but that her real name is Annie P. Miller. Winterborne also learns that their father lives in Schenectady, New York, is very rich, and doesn't like Europe.

Miss Daisy Miller explains that they should get some tutor to travel with them who could teach young Randolph, but they haven't been able to find anyone. "She addressed her new acquaintance as if she had known him a long time." She tells Winterborne that the only thing she doesn't like about Europe is the lack of society, especially gentlemen society. Schenectady and New York City had plenty of society which she enjoyed, but here in Europe, she has been unable to discover any.

Winterborne hears all of this with a certain amount of shocked amazement. "He had never yet heard a young girl express herself in just this fashion." He wonders if she is a great flirt or simply the essence of innocence. He finally decides that she is a pretty American flirt.

Daisy soon points to a nearby castle and wonders if Winterborne has seen it. She wants to go, but her mother doesn't feel up to it. Winterborne offers his assistance. He will be glad to escort Miss Miller and her mother to the castle, but Daisy thinks that her mother wouldn't like to go. Suddenly Winterborne realizes that Daisy is willing to go with him alone. When Eugenio appears, she explains to Winterborne that he is their courier and then, addressing Eugenio, says that Mr. Winterborne has promised to take her to the castle. Winterborne feels that there has been a breach of discretion and he offers to introduce Daisy Miller to his aunt, who will vouch for his character. But Daisy doesn't seem concerned. She leaves telling him that they will soon arrange a trip to the castle.

Commentary

In this story, James uses something he calls a "central intelligence" to narrate the story. This means simply that the story is about Daisy Miller, but we see Daisy through the eyes of Winterborne. Thus, Winterborne is the central intelligence (sometimes called the sentient center). In order to utilize this technique, James must set up the qualities of his narrator. Thus Winterborne is an

American who has lived most of his life in Europe. He is, therefore, more European than he is American. Being American, he will be more understanding of Daisy Miller's behavior; but at the same time, being reared in Europe, he will also be fully aware of the unconventionality of her behavior. Throughout the story, then, we will observe Daisy Miller indirectly through Winterborne's eyes.

A principal concern in most of James' fiction is the contrast of the American society and values with those found in Europe. In fact, *Daisy Miller* is one of the first works ever to investigate this particular theme. Appropriately, the novel opens in a Swiss inn which is frequented by Americans.

An early contrast is suggested by the actions of young Randolph. He is more forward than the European youths would be, and he has no qualms about approaching a stranger. When Daisy Miller does the same, we are prepared to accept this as a part of the American character. Young Randolph is also quite frank: he tells Winterborne with all sincerity that American men are better than European men. The statement was not meant as a specific compliment to Winterborne, but serves as one anyway.

It is with the appearance of Daisy Miller herself that the contrast between the two cultures or two systems of values is expanded. Daisy approaches with the confidence of a person accustomed to a certain amount of independence. Thus, two of the American qualities are those of confidence and independence. Even young Randolph has more freedom than do his European counterparts. As Daisy Miller says: "There's one boy here, but he always goes around with a teacher. They won't let him play." In contrast, young Randolph seems to have more freedom than he needs.

Some critics have superficially criticized this story as being too absurd to read in this modern age when there is naturally more freedom than was found in the nineteenth century. But even though we don't understand much of the restrictions, James is very careful to set up certain norms of behavior from which the character deviates. For example, Winterborne ponders the actions that are allowed a man in Geneva and wonders how far he can go with the American girl. His perplexity, his confusion, and his failure to understand certain qualities in Daisy Miller intimate the normal code of behavior expected of young ladies. Thus, it is quite clear to any reader just how much Daisy is exceeding the bounds of propriety.

The reader should be aware of another of James' techniques. It is James' habit to let the reader gradually learn more and more about a character. We have a brief scene in which Daisy Miller is presented, then we have a brief scene where Winterborne contemplates the meaning of the girl's behavior. Gradually then, we arrive at a conclusion about her as Winterborne investigates more and more aspects of her character. Essentially by the end of this first section, we have most of her characteristics outlined for us. The remaining three sections will simply develop these basic traits.

What then is Daisy Miller? She has a want of finish, but still radiates with a charm and innocence. Her pert little face gives no trace of irony or mockery. She responds to things with sincerity and is perfectly frank in talking about her desire for the company of gentlemen. She is not bashful even when she should be. She does not understand that she cannot do the same things in Europe that she did in Schenectady, New York. Even her language is not of the most refined type. Daisy possesses a mixture of qualities that tend to confuse poor Winterborne. He even feels that perhaps he has become morally muddled. But finally, in spite of all of Daisy Miller's innocence, he decides that she is a flirt—"a pretty American flirt." What Winterborne does not understand is that according to Daisy Miller's viewpoint, there is nothing wrong with being a flirt. In fact, in America, it is expected that a girl be something of a flirt. It all depends on how far the flirtation was carried.

At the end of the section, Eugenio seems to disapprove of the arrangements Daisy Miller has made with Winterborne, and the narrator is quick to let the courier know that he is also aware of the impropriety of the entire situation. But he is so charmed and perplexed by this unusual girl that he will allow to escape him any chance to find out more about her.

SECTION 2

Summary

Winterborne has promised too much in saying he would introduce Daisy Miller to his aunt. The aunt, Mrs. Costello, is very aloof
and aristocratic, and she does not approve of the Millers. She cannot accept them because they are so common. She has heard par-
ticularly unfavorable things about the young Miss Miller. Winterborne tries to explain that Daisy is really quite innocent but has not
yet learned all of the educated ways of the world. When he tells his
aunt that he is going to take Daisy Miller to the castle, Mrs. Costello is "honestly shocked."

When Winterborne next meets Daisy, he is concerned about
his aunt's refusal to meet her. Daisy promptly tells him that she has
been looking for his aunt. She has heard a great deal about Mrs.
Costello from the chambermaids and is quite anxious to become
acquainted with her. Winterborne tries to cover for his aunt by
saying that she is often confined to her room with headaches. Upon
further questioning, Daisy suddenly realizes that the aunt doesn't
want to know her. Then Winterborne feels like admitting that his
aunt is a "proud, rude woman and...that they needn't mind her."

Mrs. Miller appears and Daisy introduces Winterborne. Soon
Daisy mentions that she is going to visit the castle with Mr. Winterborne. When Mrs. Miller says nothing, he assumes "that she deeply
disapproved of the projected excursion." He has even taken it as a
matter of course that she would accompany them. But Mrs. Miller
simply says that the two should go alone.

Suddenly, Daisy suggests that they go for a row on the lake.
Even Mrs. Miller thinks this would not be good, but Daisy insists.
The courier appears and it is obvious that he is shocked when he
learns that Miss Miller (or any young lady) would actually go out
alone at night with a gentleman. Then just as suddenly, Daisy
changes her mind, leaving Winterborne extremely perplexed and
puzzled by her actions.

Two days later, he takes Daisy on the boat. She is extremely relaxed and yet animated. Her responses to the castle are refreshing. The day is proving to be exceptional for Winterborne until he mentions that he has to leave the next day. Immediately, Daisy tells him that he is horrid. To his bewilderment, she attributes his departure to the demands of some possessive woman. She then promises to quit "teasing" him if he will promise to come see her in Rome. Winterborne says that it is an easy promise to make because he has already accepted an invitation to visit his aunt when she goes to Rome.

That evening, Winterborne tells his aunt that he went with Daisy Miller to visit the castle. When she finds out that they went alone, she is thankful that she refused to be introduced to Miss Miller.

Commentary

Mrs. Costello is introduced as a contrast to Daisy Miller. The aunt represents the aristocratic and noble lady who emphasizes adherence to proper conduct, decorum, and all the correct forms of behavior. Her reaction to any situation would be reserved and formal, whereas Daisy's would be simple and spontaneous. For Mrs. Costello, Daisy's conduct is that of a vulgar and common person. Through the aunt's views, we are better able to realize that some of Daisy's actions are improper or in bad taste.

Mrs. Costello also serves as the *confidante* to Winterborne. James uses the confidante to help present certain aspects of the story. As in the case of Mrs. Costello, the confidante is usually separated from the main action of the story. Mrs. Costello never meets Daisy Miller, but she hears enough about her in order to express her views rather forcefully. Furthermore, she is called the confidante because the main character (Winterborne) can come to her and discuss his problems and express his views with confidence. In other words, by discussing his views with Mrs. Costello, Winterborne is better able to define his exact position.

Note that Daisy Miller is not as insensitive as at first appears. She is able to tell immediately that Mrs. Costello has refused to see her and is somewhat disturbed by the slight, but she is too involved with experiencing and enjoying life to allow this refusal to affect her response to life.

Winterborne's reaction to his aunt's refusal is also significant. Essentially, he agrees with his aunt about Daisy's deportment, but in Daisy's presence, he is captured by her charms. Thus, his views combine those of the American and those of the European. He is, furthermore, the formal man who is attracted by Daisy's spontaneity.

When Daisy attempts to introduce Winterborne to her mother, she explains that her mother doesn't like to be introduced to people and is especially shy about meeting Daisy's gentlemen friends. In contrast, a European mother would *insist* upon being introduced to a daughter's friends. Thus, we have another insight into Daisy's free behavior; she is acting with her mother's accord. Moreover, a European mother would never allow her daughter to go to the castle alone, whereas Mrs. Miller tells Daisy that it would be better if she went alone. Note, however, that even Winterborne thinks Mrs. Miller would deeply disapprove of the excursion. Here, then, we are dealing with Americans who function under a more liberal set of rules and under less formal conditions than do the Europeans.

Daisy's request to Winterborne that they go for a boat ride at night again shows her spontaneous but perplexing nature. Daisy does not allow the restrictions of social forms to inhibit her from doing something she really wants to do. Her desire to take the boat ride is a type of foreshadowing of what will later occur in Rome. Throughout the scene, it is obvious that Winterborne analyzed Daisy correctly when he thought her a flirt. She does openly flirt with Winterborne, but it is still an innocent flirtation. As Winterborne emphasizes, Daisy is not bad; she just doesn't care for all the limitations society has placed on her freedom.

After the trip to the castle, Winterborne is more confused than ever about Daisy's behavior. She is a mixture of innocence and crudity. He finds her reactions to the castle charming and spontaneous, but her "teasing" is not in the best taste. In spite of this, however, he recognizes her astuteness in surmising his reasons for leaving.

Our last view of Daisy in this section comes from Mrs. Costello. When she finds out that Daisy actually did go to the castle, she is horrified and glad that she refused to meet the girl. We have seen that the excursion in itself was an innocent affair and that nothing improper or immoral happened; consequently, we are perhaps partly prepared to criticize the set of values which condemns Daisy's behavior as improper. The question is how far can a young lady disregard the conventions of society and still retain her reputation.

SECTION 3

Summary

That winter in Rome, Winterborne speculates to his aunt about the propriety of calling on the Millers. After what happened in Switzerland, Mrs. Costello can't understand why he would want to keep up the acquaintance. Furthermore, Daisy Miller has been compromising herself by "picking up half a dozen...regular fortune-hunters." Daisy's mother apparently isn't concerned. In general, Mrs. Costello thinks that the Millers are "very dreadful people." Winterborne adds that they are ignorant but also very innocent. "Depend upon it they are not bad." Mrs. Costello still maintains they are hopelessly vulgar and should be avoided.

Winterborne is a little amazed that Daisy Miller has picked up so many acquaintances because he had hoped that he had made an impression on her. The next day he calls on an old friend and during his visit the Millers arrive. Daisy immediately reprimands him for not coming to see her. She then turns to talk with the hostess, Mrs. Walker, and tells her how mean Winterborne was for leaving her in Switzerland. She then asks Mrs. Walker if she can bring a friend (a Mr. Giovanelli) to her party. In answer, Mrs. Walker tells Mrs. Miller that she would be glad to see a family friend, but Mrs. Miller explains that she doesn't know the man. Daisy apparently picked him up somewhere. Mrs. Walker doesn't know what to do and says feebly that Daisy can bring the gentleman.

As the Millers are leaving, Daisy reveals that she is going for a walk in order to meet Mr. Giovanelli. Mrs. Walker is shocked and tells Daisy it is not safe. Daisy thinks it is, and then Mrs. Walker has to explain that it is not proper. Daisy doesn't want to do something improper and therefore asks Winterborne if he will accompany her. She then leaves with him.

While they walk, Daisy begins to tease Winterborne for not having come immediately to visit her. She tells him how much she is enjoying the society in Rome. As they approach the Pincian Gardens, Winterborne tells her that he is not going to help her find Mr. Giovanelli and that he plans to remain with her. Daisy ignores this and when Winterborne asks if she really means to speak to that man in public, Daisy doesn't understand him. He asserts his feeling that it is necessary to remain with her. Daisy again doesn't understand his meaning and tells him she never allows a gentleman to interfere with her. Winterborne advises her to listen to the right gentlemen and as they approach Mr. Giovanelli, he tells her that her new acquaintance is not the right one.

Daisy introduces the two gentlemen with perfect ease. Winterborne notices that Mr. Giovanelli is not a gentleman. He is a clever imitation but anyone with discrimination could see that he is, however, an imitation. As they walk, Daisy continues to perplex Winterborne. She is not the type one could simply dismiss as a "lawless woman"; on the other hand she certainly does not conduct herself as a young lady should.

After a few minutes, Winterborne notices Mrs. Walker in a nearby carriage motioning to him. When he goes to her, she tells him it is a pity to let Daisy Miller ruin herself. She plans to take Daisy into the carriage with her and then deposit her at home with Mrs. Miller, She calls to Daisy, who comes readily. Mrs. Walker asks her to get in, but Daisy refuses. Mrs. Walker reminds her that she is too young to ruin her reputation and that she is being talked about. Daisy is surprised and wants to know what Mrs. Walker means. She tells Daisy to get into the carriage and she will explain. Suddenly, Daisy says that she thinks she would prefer *not* to know what Mrs. Walker means. She wonders if Winterborne thinks she should get into the carriage in order to save her reputation, and Winterborne tells her directly that he thinks she should get in. Daisy then tells them that if it is improper for her to walk, then she is completely improper and they must give her up entirely. She bids them goodby and leaves.

At Mrs. Walker's request, Winterborne enters her carriage and rides with her. She tells him that Miss Miller has gone too far. Winterborne still maintains that she meant no harm and her only fault is that "she is very uncultivated." Mrs. Walker then begs Winterborne not to flirt with Daisy anymore, but he tells her that he still likes Miss Miller extremely and assures Mrs. Walker that his attentions will not evoke any scandal.

When Mrs. Walker lets Winterborne out, he notices Daisy and her companion seated some distance away in a very intimate manner. He observes her a few minutes and then walks toward his aunt's residence.

Commentary

This section opens with Winterborne hearing from Mrs. Costello that Daisy Miller is still compromising herself. Thus, we get from the aunt the distant view of Daisy before we meet her again. Winterborne still maintains that she is ignorant or innocent, but that she is not really bad.

When Daisy meets Winterborne again, she acts as though they are very old and intimate friends. In other words, she does flirt with him. Of more importance is her desire and request to bring Mr. Giovanelli to Mrs. Walker's party. If Daisy thought she were doing anything improper, she would not have made the request. But the point is that Daisy is indeed innocent. She has met someone and has responded to that person. Now she wishes to bring that person to a party. It seems a natural reaction and if it is improper, then Daisy thinks the restrictions of society are unnatural.

Furthermore, when Daisy wants to go for a walk, she sees nothing wrong about this. When Mrs. Walker objects, Daisy says she doesn't want to do anything improper, but then she proceeds to do just that. She asks Winterborne to go with her because she is more interested in living than she is in the proper forms of behavior.

While Daisy is the spontaneous person, her friend Mr. Giovanelli is aware of all the proper forms of behavior and decorum. He is extremely urbane and is able to cover his disappointment and seem even more charming in proportion to how much he is disappointed. This demeanor is just the opposite from that of Daisy Miller, who allows people to know her feelings immediately. Furthermore, Mr. Giovanelli represents the imitation of a gentleman. This again reflects on Daisy, who cannot tell the real thing from the imitation.

During the walk with Daisy and Mr. Giovanelli, Winterborne is still unable to tell what type of person Daisy actually is. She was an "inscrutable combination of audacity and innocence." She showed no awareness of shame or improper conduct and responded gaily to any event.

Mrs. Walker's intervention indicates that Daisy is certainly more concerned with life than she is in the proper forms. She knows that what she is doing is innocent and she sees no reason why she should deny herself pleasure simply to satisfy the whims of an established convention. Perhaps no sentence characterizes Daisy as well as does her comment that she does not want to know what Mrs. Walker would tell her. In other words, Daisy would rather not hear something that is unpleasant. She builds her life on enjoyment and appreciation rather than adherence to staid and set rules. She is, furthermore, quite direct and honest in saying that if she is improper for walking in public with a man, then she is completely improper and should be given up. In other words, Daisy would like people to respond to her and quit judging her. She is not immoral, but prefers to live life rather than abide by rules which seem designed to deny life.

Finally, even Winterborne questions the rules which condemn Daisy's actions. He has been with her while she was committing something improper and found her charming and innocent. Consequently, why should an innocent girl be censured for her actions? As Winterborne says to Mrs. Walker: "I suspect...that you and I have lived too long at Geneva." He means, of course, that they are too much influenced by Europeans' emphasis on proper decorum and have forgotten the spontaniety with which Americans approach life.

Summary

For the next two days, Winterborne calls on the Millers but does not find them at home. The third day was Mrs. Walker's party, which Winterborne attended. Mrs. Miller arrived by herself and told Mrs. Walker that she left Daisy *alone* with Mr. Giovanelli. Daisy had pushed Mrs. Miller out the door because she wanted to practice some singing with her new friend. Mrs. Walker is shocked and feels Daisy is intentionally being improper.

At eleven, Daisy comes bustling in with Mr. Giovanelli and gaily chats with everyone. With charming vivacity she tells Mrs. Walker that Mr. Giovanelli sings quite well. During the party, her companion conducts himself according to all the *proper* forms of behavior, while Daisy gaily chats with everyone. When she approaches Winterborne, she mentions how strange Mrs. Walker's behavior was the day before. Daisy thinks it would have been highly improper to desert Mr. Giovanelli. Winterborne explains that it was wrong for Mr. Giovanelli to ask her to walk because he "would never have proposed to a young lady of this country to walk about the streets with him." Daisy's response is that she is glad she is not a young lady of this country, for they must have a bad time of it. Winterborne tells her that her "habits are those of a flirt" and Daisy explains that all "nice girls are flirts." But she doesn't like to flirt with Winterborne because he is so stiff.

Winterborne continues to explain that Daisy's actions in public are being talked about and her reputation is in danger. Daisy responds by saying that at least Mr. Giovanelli doesn't say such unpleasant things to her. The gentleman in question arrives and offers Daisy some tea, which she accepts, observing that she prefers weak tea to good advice.

When Daisy goes to bid her hostess goodnight, Mrs. Walker intentionally turns her back and leaves Daisy "to depart with what grace she might." Winterborne observes the entire scene and sees Daisy turn "very pale." When Winterborne tells Mrs. Walker how cruel it was, she responds that Daisy will never again enter her drawing room.

26

After this, Winterborne often calls at the Millers and always finds Mr. Giovanelli there. Daisy is never upset and can converse as brightly with two men as with one. Winterborne is convinced from these visits that Daisy is very much interested in her Italian friend.

With his aunt, Winterborne admits that Daisy's actions are strange, since the young lady apparently does not want to marry and he cannot believe that Mr. Giovanelli expects it. Furthermore, Winterborne has made inquiries about "the little Italian," and discovered him to be an undistinguished lawyer.

Constantly hearing more about Daisy's many indiscretions, Winterborne decides to try approaching Mrs. Miller. Hearing one day that Daisy is riding through town alone with Mr. Giovanelli, he goes to visit Mrs. Miller. But the mother is so unconcerned that he considered his attempt futile.

Some days later, Winterborne meets Daisy and her companion in the Palace of the Caesars. Daisy thinks Winterborne is annoyed at her because she goes around so much with Mr. Giovanelli. He explains that he is not as annoyed as others are and that the others will show it by being disagreeable. She wonders why Winterborne allows people to be unkind to her. He says that he has tried to defend her by telling everyone that Daisy's mother considers her to be engaged. At first Daisy declares that she is engaged and immediately says that she is not. She then leaves with her companion.

A week later, Winterborne is returning from a party and decides to stroll into the Colosseum to see it in the moonlight. As he draws near, he hears voices, one of which he recognizes as belonging to Miss Daisy Miller. He stops and observes her and Mr. Giovanelli. Suddenly, he realizes that Daisy is "a young lady whom a gentleman need no longer be at pains to respect." As he is leaving, he hears Daisy cry out that Mr. Winterborne is cutting her.

Winterborne goes to her and reminds her of the danger of the Roman fever. He then wonders why Mr. Giovanelli countenanced such an imprudent action. The Italian explains that he told Miss

Miller it would be an indiscretion, but she insisted upon seeing the Colosseum by moonlight. Winterborne advises them to leave immediately.

As Giovanelli goes for the carriage, Daisy asks Winterborne if he still thinks of her as engaged. He tells her "it makes very little difference whether" she is engaged or not. As Daisy leaves, she seems changed and says that she does not care whether she catches the fever or not.

A few days later Winterborne hears that Daisy is sick. He goes to call at the hotel and learns that Miss Miller is seriously ill. The mother comes to him and gives him a message from Daisy. He hears that when she gained consciousness, she wanted her mother to be sure and tell Mr. Winterborne that she was not engaged. She also asked him to remember their visit to the castle in Switzerland.

A week after this, Daisy dies. At the funeral, Winterborne meets Mr. Giovanelli, who speaks of Daisy in the best terms and concludes by saying she was the most innocent person. He admits that she would have never married him, but he still admired her tremendously.

The following summer when he is visiting his aunt, Winterborne speaks of the injustice he had done to Daisy. He tells Mrs. Costello that Daisy sent him messages from her deathbed that he now understands. She would have appreciated someone's esteem. Winterborne thinks that he has indeed lived "too long in foreign parts."

Commentary

The entire last section recounts Daisy's rapid decline through showing several more of her indiscretions. We hear immediately that Daisy is alone in the apartment with Mr. Giovanelli and that she sent her mother on ahead so that she could be alone with the man. We do not know Daisy's motivations for this indiscretion, but she is certainly open about it. When she arrives at the party, she innocently tells that she remained alone in order to practice some songs. If Daisy had any concept or thought of impropriety, she would not have been so free to discuss it at the party.

Daisy apparently lives for the worth of the human being and for human relationships. In other words, she thought it would have been more improper for her to desert Mr. Giovanelli than to be seen walking with him. Simply because the ladies of Italy do not walk is no reason for Daisy to be denied this simple pleasure. As she said, she sees no reason why she should change her habits to conform to the ladies of Italy, when their habits deny most of the simple pleasure in life.

Daisy is, however, sensitive to rebuffs from others. When Mrs. Walker turns her back on Daisy, Winterborne notices that the young lady is deeply hurt. She has never been treated so rudely before and is temporarily at a loss of know how to interpret it.

As Winterborne continues to see Daisy, he realizes more and more that she is a person who likes her freedom and who likes to respond to any aspect of life without restrictions. When Winterborne visits the Millers, he is constantly aware of Daisy's "inexhaustible good humour." He knows that she prefers to have a good time to being thought of as absolutely proper. She seems to work always with an inner knowledge that she is innocent and, with innocence, one should not have to worry about one's reputation. As Daisy tells Winterborne, she prefers tea to advice, and would rather be with people who say agreeable things to her than with those who say disagreeable things.

What disappoints Winterborne is the fact that Daisy represents so much that is pretty, innocent, spontaneous, and good, but all of these qualities are being misdirected. So much that is admirable is being made ugly.

Winterborne is, of course, stultified when he attempts to speak with Mrs. Miller. Here is a mother the like of which he has never before encountered. She seems totally indifferent to her daughter's behavior. Consequently, Daisy's actions must be in accord with some new type of American behavior.

Finally, even Winterborne is shocked with Daisy. When he discovers her alone at night with Mr. Giovanelli in the Colosseum, he too admits that she need no longer be treated with respect. But this final indiscretion is paid for severely. Because of this night Daisy contracts the Roman fever and is soon dead. It is as though her final act of imprudence is equated with her death.

It is only after Daisy's death that Winterborne realizes she would have enjoyed someone's esteem. But the person to esteem her would have had to be a person who realized that she was essentially innocent and only searching for some simple but enjoyable experiences in life.

The final emphasis of the story is again on Daisy's innocence. Mr. Giovanelli maintains that she was the most wonderful and innocent person he had ever met. It is an innocence that is American and this same quality when not tempered with the proper forms of behavior will often be interpreted incorrectly. Thus, Winterborne feels that he has lived too long in Europe.

MEANING THROUGH SOCIAL CONTRASTS

Henry James was the first novelist to write on the theme of the American versus the European with any degree of success. Almost all of his major novels may be approached as a study of the social theme of the American in Europe, in which James contrasts the active life of the American with the mannered life of the European aristocray or he contrasts the free open nature of the American with the more formalized and stiff rules found in Europe. Embodied in this contrast is the moral theme in which the innocence of the American is contrasted with the knowledge and experience (and evil) of the European. *Daisy Miller* is one of James' earliest works involving this theme. All the comments presented here are not found in this work, but for the sake of James' entire theory, it is useful to see how he took some of the basic aspects found in *Daisy Miller* and used them consistently throughout his fiction.

In its most general terms, that is, in terms which will apply to almost any Jamesian novel, the contrasts as seen as follows:

THE AMERICAN		THE EUROPEAN
innocence	vs.	knowledge or experience
utility	vs.	form and ceremony
spontaneity	vs.	ritual
action	vs.	inaction
nature	vs.	art
natural	vs.	artificial
honesty	vs.	evil

The above list could be extended to include other virtues or qualities, but this list, or even half this list, will suffice to demonstrate James' theme or idea in the use of this American-European contrast.

The reader should also remember that James uses these ideas with a great deal of flexibility. It does not always hold that every European will have exactly these qualities or that every American will. Indeed, some of the more admirable characters are Europeans who possess many of these qualities and in turn lack others. Because a European might possess urbanity and knowledge and experience does not necessarily mean that he is artificial and evil. And quite the contrary, many Americans come with natural spontaneity and are not necessarily honest and admirable.

In *Daisy Miller,* James is more concerned with the difference in behavior than he is with the specific person. But generally, the character who represents the American is, of course, Daisy Miller herself. The representative of the European attitude in the worst sense of the word is Mrs. Costello, and to a lesser degree Mrs. Walker and Winterborne. Of course, all of these "Europeans" were actually born in America, but they have lived their entire lives in Europe and have adopted the European mode of viewing life.

One of the great differences that is emphasized is the difference between the American's spontaneity and the European's insistence upon form and ceremony. Daisy likes to react to any situation according to her own desires. Even though people tell her that certain things are improper, Daisy likes to do what she thinks is free and right. On the contrary, Mrs. Walker would never act in any manner except that approved by all society. The American than acts spontaneously, while the Europeans have formalized certain rituals so that they will never have to confront an unknown situation. Thus, there is a sense of sincerity in the American's actions; whereas the European is more characterized by a sense of extreme urbanity. Throughout the novel, we never see Daisy perform any action but that which is natural and open.

The American's sense of spontaneity, sincerity, and action leads him into natural actions. He seems to represent nature itself. On the other hand, the European's emphasis on form, ceremony, ritual, and urbanity seems to suggest the artificial. It represents art as an entity opposing nature.

Ultimately, these qualities lead to the opposition of honesty versus evil. This question is not investigated in *Daisy Miller,* but in terms of James' final position, it might be wise to know his final stand. When all American qualities are replaced by all of the European, we find that form and ritual supplant honesty. The ideal person is one who can retain all of the American's innocence and honesty, and yet gain the European's experience and knowledge.

THE TURN OF THE SCREW

LIST OF CHARACTERS

The Governess
Narrator of the story, who is appointed as governess of Miles and Flora with the instructions that she never bother her employer, the children's uncle.

Flora and Miles
The two children who, as orphans, are placed in the governess' charge by their uncle.

Mrs. Grose
The housekeeper and confidante to the governess.

Peter Quint
Former personal servant to the employer of the governess and familiar companion to Miles. He has been dead a year.

Miss Jessel
The children's former governess, who died the year before.

GENERAL PLOT SUMMARY

In an old house on a Christmas Eve, the subject of ghosts is brought up. A man named Douglas tells of his sister's governess, who had reported seeing apparitions some years ago; in fact, she had recorded her experience in a manuscript that he promises to send for. Upon further questioning, it is learned that the governess was hired to take care of two young pupils who had been left under the care of an uncle. When this man hired the governess, he gave her implicit instructions that she was to cope with any problem and never bother him.

The governess' story opens on the day she arrives at her new position. Her charges — Miles and Flora — are perfect little children who would apparently never cause anyone any trouble. She grows very fond of them in spite of the fact that little Miles has been discharged from his school. In discussing this occurrence, the governess and Mrs. Grose, the housekeeper, decide that little Miles was just too good for a regular school.

The governess loves her position and her children, and secretly wishes that her handsome employer could see how well she is doing. Shortly after this, she notices the form of a strange man at some distance. She wonders if the large country house harbors some secret. But some time later, she sees the same face outside the dining room window. When she describes this face to Mrs. Grose, she hears that it was that of Peter Quint, an ex-servant who has been dead for about a year.

Next the governess encounters another apparition in the form of a lady. Upon further consultation with Mrs. Grose, it is determined that this was the children's former governess, Miss Jessel, who died mysteriously about a year ago. When the present governess presses Mrs. Grose for additional information, she learns that Peter Quint and Miss Jessel had been intimate with each other and, furthermore, that both had been too familiar with the children.

After more appearances, the governess decides that the figures are returning to see the children. She then begins to wonder if the children know of the presence of the apparitions. Upon observing the children's behavior, she decides that they must be aware of the presence of these figures. She notes that once in the middle of the night little Miles is out walking on the lawn. Also, little Flora often gets up in the night and looks out the window.

Coming back early one day from church, the governess finds Miss Jessel in the schoolroom. During the confrontation, the governess feels that the former teacher wants to get Flora and make the little girl suffer with her. She is now determined to break her arrangement with her employer and write to him to come down.

Walking by the lake that day, she sees the figure of Miss Jessel again and directs little Flora's attention to it. But the little girl can see nothing. Furthermore, the housekeeper, who is along, can see nothing. Mrs. Grose takes little Flora and goes back to the house. The next day the housekeeper comes to the governess and tells of the awful language young Flora used and reasons that the girl must be in contact with some evil person in order to use such language.

The governess has little Flora taken away and that night as she is talking with little Miles, the figure of Peter Quint appears at the window. When the governess confronts little Miles with this apparition, the boy collapses and the governess notes that he is dead.

SUMMARIES AND COMMENTARIES

"PROLOGUE"

Summary

A group of visitors are gathered around a fireplace discussing the possible horror of a ghost appearing to a young, innocent child. A man named Douglas wonders if *one* child "gives the effect another turn of the screw," what would a story involving a ghostly visitation to two children do? Everyone wants to hear his story, but Douglas explains that he must send for a manuscript. The story he wants to relate was narrated by a governess who has been dead twenty years. She was once his sister's governess and Douglas has heard the story firsthand.

When the group has heard more about the governess, everyone wonders if she was in love. Douglas admits that she was and that the beauty of her love was that she saw the man she loved only twice. He was her employer and had hired her on the condition that she never trouble him, "never appeal nor complain nor write about anything," and that she was to handle all problems herself. In other words, she was to take complete charge of the two children to be placed under her authority.

Commentary

In this introductory section—note that James does not call it a prologue—we are given just the bare essentials of the story. It will be left for the manuscript, that is, the governess, to tell the main story. The only outside or objective facts we have in the entire narrative come from this section. But at the same time, we must be aware that these come from Douglas, who is accused of having been in love with the governess, and thus his view may be colored.

SECTION 1

Summary

After having come to an agreement with the uncle of the two children and fully understanding that he does not wish to be bothered in any way with the upbringing of his wards, the governess takes a carriage to the great country house. Here she meets the first of her two pupils. Young Flora, a child of eight, is "so charming as to make it a great fortune to have to do with her." She is the most beautiful child the governess has ever seen.

On the way to the great country house, the governess had brooded over her future relationship with the housekeeper, but upon meeting Mrs. Grose, it is obvious that they would have an excellent understanding.

The governess is so charmed by young Flora that she takes the first possible opportunity to question Mrs. Grose about young Miles, her second pupil. She learns that the little boy, who is two years older that his sister, is as charming and delightful as Flora. He is to arrive in two days from his boarding school.

Commentary

The reader should remember constantly that the governess is now narrating the story and that all impressions and descriptions come from her viewpoint. Thus, to the governess, young Flora appears as the most charming young girl she has ever seen. We should now go back and speculate about the possible relationship between the governess and her employer. As the governess tells Mrs. Grose: "I was carried away in London!" As the simple daughter of a country parson, the young girl has been impressed by the elegance and free manner of her employer. Thus, some critics would suggest that the governess' view of the young girl is simply a sub-conscious desire to see everything connected with her employer as beautiful and wonderful. Other critics suggest that James is here establishing the beauty and innocence of the young girl, which will later be used in various ways.

It is likewise important to note that the governess and Mrs. Grose become immediate friends and agree basically on most things. This rapport will allow the governess to convince Mrs. Grose later of the possibility of ghosts.

SECTION 2

Summary

Shortly before young Miles is to arrive home from school, the governess receives a letter from her employer. It contains an un-opened letter from the headmaster of Miles' school and a cursory note from her employer requesting her to open the letter and attend to all details. Above all, she is not to trouble him.

After reading the letter, the governess searches out Mrs. Grose and reports that Miles has been dismissed from his school. She inquires if young Miles is "really bad," and is assured by Mrs. Grose that young Miles is incapable of injuring anyone, even though he is a lively young boy.

At her next meeting with Mrs. Grose, the governess inquires about her predecessor. She hears that the earlier governess was not careful in all things, and after leaving the last time on her vacation, was suddenly taken ill and died. Mrs. Grose knows no more particulars, and the governess must be content with this incomplete report.

Commentary

The first strange element is now introduced into the story. Miles, we find out, has been suspended from his school and will not be allowed to return. This dismissal immediately brings to the fore-front the possibility of his being a bad boy. "Is he really bad?" the governess asks, and the idea is given further significance by the later use of words "contaminate" and "corrupt."

The idea of death is also introduced here as the governess discovers that her predecessor left with the intentions of returning and then was taken ill and died. The cause of her death is left unexplained, thereby adding a note of mystery to it.

SECTION 3

Summary

As soon as the governess sees young Miles, she thinks him to possess the same exceptional qualities, with the "same positive fragrance of purity" that characterize young Flora. She soon lets Mrs. Grose know that Miles' dismissal must have been a cruel charge. Furthermore, she has decided to ignore the letter and will not even write to the boy's uncle about the incident.

In the first weeks of her duties, the children are wonderful; "they were of a gentleness so extraordinary." But in spite of the pleasure the governess has in the presence of the two children, she still treasures her free time, which falls late in the afternoon, between daylight and darkness. She often strolls through the grounds and meditates on the beauty of her surroundings. Sometimes, she thinks that it would be charming to suddenly meet someone on the path who would stand before her "and smile and approve." In fact, she wishes her employer could know how much she enjoys the place and how well she is executing her duties.

One evening during her stroll, she does perceive the figure of a strange man on top of one of the old towers of the house. He appears rather indistinct, but she is aware that he keeps his eyes on her. She feels rather disturbed without knowing why.

Commentary

The innocence of both children is further emphasized in this section. The governess perhaps makes her first mistake in refusing to investigate the causes of Miles' dismissal. The mystery connected with this suspension will later allow the governess to attribute a duplicity to Miles' actions. The governess' refusal to investigate stems from her overzealous desire to exercise complete control over her wards and to view them in her own way.

Note how carefully James sets up the machinery for the governess' first sight of the "ghosts." Her free time falls at dusk, and at this time she usually likes to wander around alone. Furthermore, on her walks, she wishes that her employer could see her in this environment and would commend her upon her excellent performance with the children. In other words, it seems obvious that the governess is attracted or infatuated by her employer. Whether or not this infatuation is strong enough or psychotic enough to allow the governess to "create" the ghosts must be determined by each individual reader. Many critics have suggested that the ghosts are only creations of the governess' imagination, evoked to compel her employer to come to the country house. Whatever the circumstances, the governess' wish to meet someone on her walks is soon fulfilled, since she sees in the distance some strange figure standing and observing her.

SECTIONS 4, 5

Summary

After seeing the person (or apparition), the governess wonders if there was a "secret at Bly" (Bly is the name of the country house). She spends a good portion of the succeeding days thinking about this encounter. The shock has "sharpened all" her senses, and she fears that she might become too nervous to keep her wits about her.

The children occupy most of her day, and she continues to discover new and exciting things about them. The only obscurity which persists is the boy's conduct at school which had brought about his dismissal. The governess finds him to be an angel and decides that he was too good for the public school. Even though things are not well at the governess' own home, she has no complaints about her work.

One Sunday as the group is preparing to go to church, the governess returns to the dining room to retrieve her gloves from the table. Inside the room she notices the strange weird face of a man staring in at her in a hard and deep manner. Suddenly she realizes that the man has "come for someone else." This thought gives her courage, and she goes immediately to the outside. Once there she finds nothing, but looking through the window, she sees Mrs. Grose, who upon seeing the governess outside the glass, turns pale from fright.

In a moment, Mrs. Grose appears outside the house and tells the governess how white she is. The governess explains that just a moment before she saw the figure of a man standing on the outside looking in. She reports having seen him one time before. It is settled that the man is no gentleman, in fact the governess calls him "a horror." She refuses to go to church with the others because she is afraid—not for herself but for the children.

When Mrs. Grose asks for a description of the stranger, the governess is able to give a rather minute and detailed account of him. His red hair, his thin but good features, and his clothes remind her of some actor who is imitating some other person. Even though he was dressed in clothes a gentleman would wear, he was indeed no gentleman. Mrs. Grose immediately seems to recognize the person described and explains that the man was dressed in the master's clothes. He is Peter Quint, who was once the master's personal valet and who wore the master's clothes. When the governess wonders what happened to the ex-valet, she is told that he died.

Commentary

Section 4 opens with the mystery of some secret at Bly. This secret is built up in the governess' mind and she thinks about it until later she sees the figure at the window. Again, the climate combines to help add mystery to the appearance. The figure appears on a cold, gray day. There are several ways of approaching the appearance of Peter Quint. Some critics maintain that the ghost is a product of the governess' imagination, and she sees him only because she has been brooding on the subject for so long that her mind actually creates a figure. This point is supported by the fact that the governess knows the type of clothes that her employer wears and has constantly desired another view of him; thus in her imagination, she has created a person looking handsome but, as in dreams, appearing rather horrible also. This person then is in some ways the dream fulfillment and exists only in the governess' imagination.

The other point of view is that the governess could not give such an exact description if she had not actually seen the ghost. In this view, the governess is seen as a pure and innocent person who is the guardian of the pure and innocent children. In these two sections, great pains have been taken to emphasize once again the natural purity and sweetness of the two children. Therefore, the ghost could be symbolic of evil approaching upon innocence and the struggle such an encounter must involve.

Thus, through the use of ambiguity, James has left room for more than one view of the situation. There are even a few critics who maintain that this story is nothing more than a pure, chilling ghost story and has no meaning beyond this reading.

SECTIONS 6, 7

Summary

Mrs. Grose accepted what the governess had to say about the appearance of the stranger without questioning anything. The governess knows what she herself is capable of to shelter her pupils, and she tells the housekeeper that the apparition was looking for little Miles. She cannot explain how she knows this, but she is sure of it. She suddenly remembers that neither of the pupils has even mentioned Peter Quint's name to her. Mrs. Grose states that Quint often took great liberties with the child. In fact, she adds, he was too free with everyone. The governess then wants to know if everyone knew that Quint was admittedly bad. Mrs. Grose knew about him, but the master suspected nothing; and she never presumed to inform, since the master didn't take well to people who bore tales and bothered him. And actually, she was afraid of what Peter Quint could do. The governess is shocked because she thinks that one would be more afraid of what effect this evil person might have on the innocent life of the young boy than of what the master or Quint would do.

During the next week, Mrs. Grose and the governess talk incessantly of the appearance of this sinister figure. The governess learns that he had fallen on ice while coming home drunk from a tavern and was later found dead. Through it all, the governess discovers that she has more strength than ever and is more determined to protect her pupils from any danger.

Soon after, the governess and little Flora are out by the lake when a figure appears standing on the opposite side, observing them. The governess watches to see if little Flora will take notice of the figure. She is certain that the girl sees it and only pretends to be oblivious to it.

As soon as possible, the governess finds Mrs. Grose and explains that the children know of the presence of these other beings. Mrs. Grose is horrified and wants to know why the governess has come to such a conclusion. The governess explains that she was with Flora on the bank when Miss Jessel, Flora's previous governess, who died last year, appeared on the other side. Mrs. Grose is horrified and can't believe it. She wants to know how the governess was able to determine that it was Miss Jessel. The governess explains that by the way Miss Jessel looked so intently at little Flora and by the grand beauty and lady-like presence but at the same time an infamous quality that exuded from her. Then Mrs. Grose admits that Miss Jessel, in spite of her position, was familiar with Peter Quint. It is suggested that when she left her position, she couldn't return, but Mrs. Grose doesn't know exactly what Miss Jessel died of.

Suddenly, the governess realizes that she can't shield or protect the young children because she fears that they are already lost.

Commentary

In the discussion with Mrs. Grose, the governess discovers that the housekeeper knew Peter Quint was evil, but she was afraid to tell the master because he did not like to be bothered by details and complaints and he was impatient with people who bore tales against their fellow workers. Consequently, the governess is again reminded that she is in complete charge of her pupils and will not be able to go to the master with any complaint.

With the appearance of Miss Jessel, James is rounding out his story. The male ghost appears for the boy, and the female apparently returns for the young girl. The governess finds herself trapped in the middle.

We should be aware in this section that not as much credence is given to the appearance of Miss Jessel. There is even a bit of doubt in the mind of good Mrs. Grose. It is almost as though the governess' mind has brooded on the subject until she creates the appearance of Miss Jessel. There is not the direct description which will allow Mrs. Grose to positively identify the former governess, and the details given could apply to almost any governess.

Another level of meaning is added here. The governess thinks that the apparitions are returning to capture or corrupt the children. As long as she thinks this, then she is ready to fight diligently in order to protect the children. Her fears are made more real when she learns that both Peter Quint and Miss Jessel were immoral people. She is already afraid that the mere presence of these people in real life might have had a corrupting influence on the children. Thus, in their spectral appearance, they want to continue the corruption began in life.

The most horrifying thing for the governess is the conviction that the children know of the presence of the ghosts and pretend not to know it. Here we must begin to wonder if the governess is not letting her imagination carry her away. Even if the ghosts do appear, it is quite plausible that little Flora did not notice the figure which was, indeed, at some distance. But if the ghosts are real, then we must admire the governess, who is determined to protect her wards against the evil influence.

SECTIONS 8, 9, 10

Summary

At a later time, the governess has a talk with the housekeeper, when they agree that the governess couldn't make up the story because she had given such a perfect description, even to the last detail, of the two characters. In the meantime, the governess has devoted herself to her pupils, who have been more than charming —they have been perfect.

The governess cannot forget that Miles was discharged from his school. Therefore, one day she decides to question Mrs. Grose about him. She wonders if he has ever been bad. Mrs. Grose responds that she could not like a boy that did not sometimes show signs of typical badness. Upon being pressed further, she does admit that once Miles was very bad to her. Mrs. Grose had suggested that the young boy was stepping beyond his position by having so much to do with Quint, and the young child reminded her that she was also a servant and no better than Quint. Furthermore, he lied to her about how much time he actually did spend with Peter Quint.

It is brought out that the previous year, young Miles spent an exceptionally large amount of time with Quint, and during this time Flora was alone with Miss Jessel. Thus, the governess thinks it is quite possible that the young children knew what was taking place between Quint and Jessel.

The governess decides to do nothing but wait and see what should happen. She waits a long time before another incident occurs. One night, she wakes up at about one o'clock, and taking her candle, goes to the stairs. Halfway down the staircase, she sees the figure of Peter Quint standing at one of the landings. She faces him directly until he retreats into the darkness. She feels that he knew her just as well as she knew him. After he has disappeared, she returns to her room. She knows that she left the candle burning and now it is out. Immediately she notices that little Flora is at the window. When she questions the child suspiciously, little Flora says that she awakened and felt that the governess had gone and she was watching to see if the governess was outside walking. The young woman wonders if she saw anyone, but little Flora innocently answers that she saw no one. When the governess tries to trap the girl by asking why she pulled the curtain over the bed to conceal her absence, little Flora simply says that she didn't want to frighten the governess. Everything seemed perfectly natural to her.

For many days after this, the governess again goes to the staircase, but never again sees Quint. Once on one of her walks, she sees the back of a woman's figure bent over as though in heavy mourning.

One night the governess awakens to find that little Flora is again missing from her bed. This time she notices that the young girl is seemingly talking to someone outside the window. Rather than confront the girl directly, the governess decides to go to Miles' room and then changes her mind because this act could be awkward. Instead, she goes to a room above, where she can view all the actions. As she peers out the window, the thing that most strikes her is the figure of poor little Miles out on the lawn by himself.

Commentary

In this story dealing with the ghostly element, we are obliged to examine the governess' fortitude. If the ghosts are real, how does she have the courage and perseverance to meet them time and time again. After all, she is a rather helpless female, and even the love that she had earlier felt for the children is not modified by her belief that they are in the confidence of the ghosts. Only a more noble urge to rescue them from the evil influence could justify the governess' actions.

Thus, can we view the entire tale as the conflict between good and evil with the governess representing the forces of good while the so-called ghosts represent something of the evil nature of the world from which the governess wishes to protect the children, while finding it impossible to do so. In this section, the innocence of the children is again emphasized. But then, if the children are actually innocent, what the governess is committing is perhaps the most neurotic and horrible of all perversions. That is, she is compromising the innocence of the children by insisting upon the actual appearance of the ghosts.

Again, the subject of Miles' dismissal from the school comes up. The mistake that the governess made was not in learning the exact nature of his dismissal. Thus she is able to conjecture about the possible reasons. She goes to Mrs. Grose and elicits information about Miles' past behavior. The housekeeper reveals that Miles had once been bad in protecting Peter Quint. But then the realistic reader would expect any boy to prefer the rough companionship of a man to that of acting the role of the gentleman at so young an age.

In these chapters, the reader should note how the governess suggests certain meanings to Mrs. Grose, who then accepts the suggestion as fact. This aspect lends credence to the view that the governess imagines much of what happens and then convinces the more simple Mrs. Grose.

A large portion of these chapters is devoted to relating additional meetings with apparitions. By now, the reader should be aware that the governess meets these figures at a time or place where it would be impossible for anyone else to confirm the phenomena. Thus, there is an ambiguity about each appearance.

The last appearance of Miss Jessel was made for the benefit of little Flora, that is according to the governess. She is convinced that Flora is talking with a strange presence and goes to investigate. During her investigation, she notices young Miles walking out on the lawn. From this observation, she will draw many conclusions, but the reader should be aware that she did *not* see either Miles or Flora in direct communication with the apparitions.

SECTIONS 11, 12

Summary

After the recent incidents, the governess keeps close watch on her charges. She feels as though she could not withstand the pressure of these days if it were not for the comfort of Mrs. Grose, who apparently believes the governess' story without reservation. Even though Mrs. Grose is a good woman, she is lacking in imagination and thus could not comprehend fully the extent of the implications involved in the present danger. Thus, the governess has to explain the meaning of last night's escapades.

As soon as she saw Miles in the yard, the governess went to the terrace, where Miles was able to see her. He came directly to her. Using the direct approach, she asked the reason for his being out on the lawn so late at night. Little Miles told her he did it so she would think him bad. His simple and sweet explanation was followed immediately by a genuine kiss.

Miles explained how he had arranged the matter with Flora. His sister was to get up and look out the window. In this way the governess would be aroused and would then see him.

After completing her narration of the preceding night to Mrs. Grose, the governess suggests that the children talk to Quint and Miss Jessel all the time. She realizes that neither pupil has even made an allusion to their old friends. She concludes that her pupils belong to them and not to her.

Mrs. Grose is shocked and wonders why "Quint and that woman" continue to return. "What can they now do?" she asks. The governess explains that they return simply "for the love of all the evil that, in those dreadful days, the pair put into them." And unless something is done, the children will be destroyed. Mrs. Grose wants the governess to write immediately to the children's uncle and have him come down to solve the situation. The governess is horrified at this suggestion and reminds Mrs. Grose that the master does not like to be bothered and that he might think the story to be some "fine machinery [she] had set in motion to attract his attention to her slighted charms." So she tells Mrs. Grose that the master is *not* to be disturbed. In fact, she would leave immediately if he were informed of the present difficulties.

Commentary

These chapters are devoted partially to exploring the relationship between the governess and Mrs. Grose. We find out that Mrs. Grose is a good-natured woman who is lacking in imagination, insight, and intuition. Accordingly, she accepts the governess' interpretation of any event. She is too amiable and simple to question the governess' view. Every conclusion that is made about the predicament comes from the governess. Mrs. Grose merely acquiesces.

The most significant revelation found in this section is the governess' attitude toward her employer and her apprehension that he might regard the entire story as a contrivance on her part to attract him. When we step back from the immediate events, we must realize that if the ghostly appearance were in actuality true, then the governess should definitely inform her master. Her refusal to do so indicates that even she partially recognizes that the ghosts could be emanations of her warped imagination. Certainly if they were real, she should acknowledge that she alone does not possess the power to contend with them. In this situation, Mrs. Grose is definitely correct in thinking the master must be informed. The governess' refusal to agree must arouse suspicion as to her motivations.

SECTIONS 13, 14, 15

Summary

In the ensuing days, the governess often thinks that her pupils are conspiring against her, and she wonders when they would openly admit that they know about Miss Jessel and Peter Quint. Sometimes she wants to cry out: "They're here, they're here, you little wretches ...and you can't deny it now." But her charges do deny it with all of their sweetness and obedience.

For many days, the governess spends as much time as possible in the presence of the children. As she tells Mrs. Grose, she feels safe as long as she also has the gift of seeing the ghosts. She believes that she must constantly observe, since it has not yet been definitely proved that the children have really seen the ghosts. But at the same time, she is unable to reject the idea that whatever she saw, "Miles and Flora saw *more*."

Often in the classroom, Flora and Miles write letters to their uncle requesting him to come for a visit, but the governess never allows these to be sent. She explains that the letters are "charming literary exercises."

While walking to church one Sunday, Miles surprises the governess by asking when he will be allowed to go back to school. He does not consider it good for a little boy to be always in the company of a lady, even though that lady is ideal. He wants to know what his uncle has done about his return to school and thinks that he should write to his uncle soon if something is not done.

The manner in which little Miles insists upon returning to school shocks the governess so much that she is not able to attend the church services. Instead, she returns to Bly. Upon entering the schoolroom, she finds herself in the presence of Miss Jessel, who is seated at the governess' desk as though she has more right to be there than did the present governess. Drawing upon all of her strength, the governess addresses the intruder directly, saying: "You terrible, miserable woman." In an instant, she has "cleared the air" and she is alone in the room with the sense that she must stay at Bly and fight against this evil influence.

Commentary

In Section 13, the governess strikes a note of contradiction. She first admits that it's not yet definitely proved that the children are aware of the ghosts, and then a moment later, expresses the fear that Miles and Flora see more (that is, more of the ghosts and more of the hidden meaning) than she does.

The subject of the uncle's appearance is further developed in these sections. First, there are the letters the children write but which are never sent. Then comes Miles' demand that his uncle be consulted about his schooling. As much as the governess wants her employer to be pleased with her and to come to Bly, she is still frightened of the possibility that he actually will appear.

It is, therefore, while under the pressure of Miles' demand and the subconscious desire to see her employer that the governess once again sees the ghost of Miss Jessel. This time, the ghost appropriately appears in the schoolroom, which suggests there is a connection between Miles' demand for more schooling and the appearance of Miss Jessel in the schoolroom.

Again the reader should note that the apparition appears to the governess when the house is completely deserted. Thus, she is again the only one who sees the ghost. Furthermore, she sees it when her mind is most troubled by difficult problems that she must solve or else break her agreement with her employer.

The conversation between Miles and the governess about his schooling rings with enough ambiguity to allow the governess to think that little boy is being extremely astute and that he is implying deeper and more threatening meaning. Yet a careful reading of the conversation shows that there is nothing more ambiguous than the actual desire of a young boy to return to normal schooling.

SECTIONS 16, 17

Summary

When the others return from church, they make no mention of the governess' absence. At teatime, the governess questions Mrs. Grose and discovers it was little Miles' idea that nothing be said. The governess tells how she returned to meet "a friend" (Miss Jessel) and to talk with her. She informs Mrs. Grose that Miss Jessel "suffers the torments...of the lost. Of the damned." The governess claims that her predecessor confessed this and also stated that she wants little Flora to share the torments with her.

After this discovery, the governess decides that she must write to the uncle and insist he come down and assume responsibility for the entire predicament. In addition, she now concludes that little Miles must have been expelled from his school for wickedness.

That night, the governess begins the letter to her employer. Leaving her room for a moment, she walks to little Miles' door. Even though it is late in the night, he calls for her to come in. She discovers that he is lying awake worrying about "this queer business" of theirs. The governess thinks he means the business about the ghosts, but little Miles quickly adds that he means this business about how he is being brought up. He emphasizes again his desire to return to a normal school, and the governess tells him that she has already written his uncle. She then implores him to let her help him. In answer to her plea, there comes a big gush of wind through the window. Little Miles shrieks and when the governess recovers her composure, she notices that the candle is out. Little Miles confesses that he blew it out.

Commentary

By teatime, the governess is able to approach Mrs. Grose and tell her that "it's now all out" between her and Miles. She then describes her meeting with Miss Jessel. It is important here to note the discrepancies between the presentation of the meeting in the last chapter and governess' narration of it to Mrs. Grose. In the actual meeting, the apparition disappeared immediately after the governess spoke to it. But in her explanation to Mrs. Grose, the governess maintains Miss Jessel said she suffers torments and that she has come back to get little Flora to share in her suffering.

This divergence could be a clue to the interpretation of the novel. The governess could be seen as the exceptionally intuitive and perceptive person who can fathom the meaning of any situation by her sensitive awareness. Or else, she is deliberately creating a situation which will allow her to write her employer. It could be argued that she has slowly been developing her case and slowly convincing Mrs. Grose so that when the employer arrives, Mrs. Grose will be able to confirm the fantastic story.

Furthermore, the governess finally convinces Mrs. Grose that Miles must have been expelled for *wickedness,* since he has no other flaw or fault that could warrant expulsion. Thus, we can see now the governess' motivation in not investigating the real reasons for Miles' dismissal. She is now able to use it for her own machinations.

If the governess is absorbed with her bizarre plot, it becomes even more natural and remarkable that little Miles should want to leave. He must feel—as he does emphasize—the strangeness of his position with the governess. After the interview in his room, he becomes even more sensitive and taut over their peculiar relationship. We should be aware that James is now building for little Miles' death at the end of the story, a death that will result from the governess' weird behavior.

SECTIONS 18, 19, 20

Summary

The next day, the governess tells Mrs. Grose that the letter to the master is written, but she fails to mention that she has not yet mailed it. That day, Miles is exceptionally kind to the governess. He even volunteers to play the piano for her. Suddenly the governess asks where Flora is. Little Miles does not know, so she assumes that Flora is with Mrs. Grose. To her consternation, she discovers that the good housekeeper has not seen Flora.

Then, the governess understands that Flora is with that woman. Also, little Miles is probably with Quint; and all the time he was being nice to the governess, he was simply covering up so that Flora could escape. Together with Mrs. Grose, the young woman goes straight to the lake in search of little Flora. The governess is convinced that the children are in communication with that awful pair and, moreover, "they say things, that, if we heard them, would simply appall us."

On arriving at the lake, they discover that Flora has apparently taken the boat and gone to the other side. Mrs. Grose is dumbfounded that such a small girl could manage a boat alone, but the governess reminds her that Flora is not alone — that woman is with her.

They walk around the lake and find Flora, who meets them with her sweet gaiety. When the child asks where Miles is, the governess in turn asks little Flora, "Where is Miss Jessel?" Immediately upon hearing this question, Mrs. Grose utters a loud sound, which causes the governess to look up and see the figure of Miss Jessel standing on the other side of the lake. She points out this figure for both Mrs. Grose and little Flora, but the young pupil keeps her eyes glued on the governess. Mrs. Grose is unable to see anything in spite of the governess' explicit directions. After a few moments, Mrs. Grose addresses little Flora and tells her then there is no one there. "It's all a mere mistake and a worry and a joke." She wants to take little Flora home as fast as possible.

Suddenly, the young girl cries out that she did not see anyone and never has. She wants to be taken away from the governess, who has been so cruel and frightening. Mrs. Grose takes the child and returns to the house. The governess is left alone to realize that the apparition appears only to the children and to herself. This will make it more difficult for her now. When she returns to the house, she finds that little Flora's things have been removed from the room.

Commentary

Here we have the revealing chapters concerning the appearance of the ghosts. Previously, the ghosts have appeared only when the governess is alone, but now Miss Jessel appears while Mrs. Grose is present. But the good housekeeper is unable to see the apparition. Consequently, the reader may now doubt seriously that the visitation has any existence except in the mind of the governess. The question arises as to whether she actually sees them. We know that the mind can convince itself that such things happen.

Another approach is to accept the governess' view that one must possess a certain amount of perception before one can discover the presence of the evil ghosts. But if we accept this view, we must also see the children as possessed of superhuman cunning and ingenuity. And note that little Flora seems distraught by the accusations made by the governess.

SECTIONS 21, 22

Summary

Early the next morning, Mrs. Grose comes to the governess' room and tells her that little Flora was "so markedly feverish that an illness was perhaps at hand." All of Flora's fears are directed against the governess. She is afraid of seeing her again, and pleads to be spared the sight of the governess.

The governess asks if Flora still persists in saying that she has seen nothing. She believes that those creatures have made the child so clever that now little Flora can go to her uncle and make the governess "out to him the lowest creature — !" The governess believes that it is best for Mrs. Grose to take the child away from the region, and in that way, she might be saved. Then the young woman will devote herself to saving little Miles.

The governess suddenly wonders if Mrs. Grose has seen something that makes her believe. The housekeeper tells her that she has seen nothing but has heard a great deal. Little Flora has used terrible language and awful words that could only be learned from some very evil source. Thereupon the governess considers herself justified in the belief that little Flora learned such words from the corrupt Miss Jessel. In answer to the governess' direct question as to whether Mrs. Grose now believes in the ghosts, the housekeeper concedes that she does.

It is then agreed that Mrs. Grose will take little Flora to London. She is warned that the master will know something because of the governess' letter. Mrs. Grose then tells the governess that the letter has disappeared. Both assume that Miles has stolen it and perhaps this was the offense he committed which brought about his expulsion. The governess hopes that in being alone with her, the boy will confess and then be saved.

The next day, Miles cannot understand how his sister was taken ill so suddenly. But he seems to accept the fact that she was sent away to keep from becoming worse because of the bad influence around Bly.

Commentary

The fact that little Flora is seriously ill suggests again the very innocence of the girl. However much she might be able to pretend on some subjects, it would be quite difficult to feign a feverish sickness. In other words, she must be deeply repulsed by the behavior of the governess. The reader should note how concerned the governess is with the possibility that the employer will hear everything from Flora, who will make the governess out to be "the lowest creature." Most of her actions are designed to influence or impress her employer. In the ensuing days, she hopes to bring Miles to her side and then she will be able to convince the master of the rightness of her actions.

Mrs. Grose is convinced of Flora's evilness simply because the little girl has used some bad words. The child's behavior is easily explainable when we consider that Miles, while away at the school, must have picked up some bad words and could have passed them on to Flora. But for the genteel Mrs. Grose who is, in fact, rather old, these words sound horrible and wicked when spoken by the child, and on this proof, she is willing to accept the premises that the girl could only learn them from an evil influence.

Little Flora's illness acts as a method of foreshadowing and preparing for Miles' reaction in the final sections. If the suggestion of the appearance of a ghost makes Flora ill, then in the next sections, the governess' actions could be too much for the nerves of the young boy.

SECTIONS 23, 24

Summary

After Flora is gone, Miles joins the governess, and they talk about how they are alone. The governess explains that she stayed to be with and help Miles. She reminds him that she is willing to do anything for him, and he promises that he will tell her anything she wants to know. First, she asks him if he took the letter she had written to his uncle. The boy readily admits that he took it and opened it in order to see what she had written about him. He further admits that he found out nothing and burned the letter.

The governess asks him if he stole letters at his school or did he take other things. Miles explains that he said certain bad things to his friends, who must have said the same things to other friends until it all got back to the masters. Just as the governess is about to insist on knowing what he said, she sees the apparition of Peter Quint at the window. She hears Miles ask if it is Miss Jessel, but she forces him to admit that it is Peter Quint who is at the window. He turns suddenly around to look and falls in her arms. The governess clutches him, but instead of a triumph, she discovers that she is holding Miles' dead body.

Commentary

Somewhere little Miles had learned some naughty or evil words. It is quite possible that he had earlier learned them from his association with Peter Quint. He repeated these words at school and when others in turn repeated them, little Miles was expelled from school. Furthermore, this accounts for little Flora's learning the awful words she used to describe the governess. During this interview with Miles, the governess thinks that she sees Peter Quint at the window. Miles' first question is to ask if she sees Miss Jessel. This question seems to attest to his innocence. In other words, he must have learned from Flora (even though it is thought by Mrs. Grose that the brother and sister had not seen each other) that the governess thinks she had seen Miss Jessel. Otherwise, the young boy would not have immediately thought that the apparition seen by the governess was Miss Jessel. It is upon the mention that the apparition is a male that the young Miles associates it with Peter Quint. But whereas the fright of a ghost had caused little Flora to become ill, it is the instrument of little Miles' death.

The last section lends great support to regarding the story as a psychological study of the governess' mind. If the ghost were real or if little Miles were in communication with the ghost, the only way to account for his death is to admit that the ghosts and their evil ways have conquered the young boy. But it seems more reasonable to assume that the ghost was visible only to the governess, and through her psychotic imagination, she simply frightened the young boy to death.

THE MEANING OF *THE TURN OF THE SCREW*

There is no story in literature which has produced such a variety of interpretations. The forgoing commentaries are accordingly based upon certain facts which could be taken in more ways than one, but lean essentially toward a psychological interpretation of the story. No understanding of this story is complete then without the knowledge of certain central critical articles written about it.

The reader interested in various approaches should consult the following important articles:

For the Freudian, or psychological, interpretation, see:

Edna Kenton, "Henry James to the Ruminant Reader: *The Turn of the Screw," The Arts* (November, 1924), pp. 245-55.

Edmund Wilson, "The Ambiguity of Henry James," *Hound and Horn,* VII (April-June, 1934), 385-406.

For an interpretation in which the governess is seen as an instrument fighting against evil as represented by the ghosts, see:

Robert Heilman, "The Turn of the Screw as Poem," *The University of Kansas City Review, XIV (Summer, 1948). 277-89.*

These articles (plus others) are collected in *A Casebook on Henry James's "The Turn of the Screw,"* edited by Gerald Willen.

SPECIAL PROBLEMS
AND INTERESTS

CENTRAL INTELLIGENCE
AND POINT-OF-VIEW

One of James' contributions to the art of fiction is in his use of point-of-view. By point-of-view is meant the angle from which the story is told. For example, previous to James' novels, much of the fiction of the day was being written from the author's viewpoint, that is, the author was telling the story and he was directing the reader's response to the story. Much of the fiction of the nineteenth century had the author as the storyteller, and the author would create scenes in which certain characters would be involved, but all of the scenes would not necessarily have the same characters in them.

James' fiction differs in his treatment of point-of-view. He was interested in establishing a central person about whom the story revolved, or else a central person who could observe and report the action. Usually, the reader would have to see all the action of the story through this character's eyes. Thus, while the central character in Daisy Miller is Daisy herself, we see her through the eyes of the "central intelligence," that is, through the eyes of Winterborne. Sometimes the central character will also be the central intelligence, as happens in *The Turn of the Screw*. In James' fiction we respond to events as the "central intelligence" would respond to them.

Furthermore, every scene in a James work has the central character present or else is a scene in which some aspect of the central character is being discussed by the central intelligence. So if Daisy is not present, the discussion is about some aspect of Daisy's character.

CONFIDANT

James wrote fiction in an era before the modern technique of the "stream-of-consciousness" was established. In the modern technique, the author feels free to go inside the mind of the character. But in James' time, this was not yet an established technique. Since James as a novelist wanted to remain outside the novel — that is, wanted to present his characters with as much objectivity and realism as possible — he created the use of a confidant.

The confidant is a person of great sensibility or sensitivity to whom the main character reveals his or her innermost thoughts (as long as they are within the bounds of propriety). The confidant is essentially a listener and in some cases an adviser. This technique of having a confidant to whom the main character can talk serves a double function. First of all, it allows the reader to see what the main character is thinking, and second, it gives a more rounded view of the action. For example, after something has happened to the main character, the confidant hears about it and in the discussion of the event, we, the readers, see and understand the various subtle implications of this situation more clearly.

The confidant is also a person who is usually somewhat removed from the central action. For example, Mrs. Costello never meets Daisy Miller but she serves as a listener to Winterborne and offers her own view about Daisy. Likewise, Mrs. Grose in *The Turn of the Screw* has never seen any of the apparitions, but she serves as the person to whom the governess expresses her doubts and fears. Thus, essentially the confidant observes the action from a distance, comments on this action, and is usually a person of some exceptional qualities who allows the main character to respond more deeply and subtly to certain situations.

FORESHADOWING

James is a very careful artist who uses rather often and freely the technique of foreshadowing a later action. This means that he has given hints in the early parts of the novel about some important thing that is going to happen later in the story. Thus, a touch of realism is added to the novel because so many things have foreshadowed the main action that the reader should not be surprised to discover the action at the end.

For example, in *Daisy Miller* we are given very early in the novel hints of Daisy's spontaneous and impetuous nature. Thus it is not surprising to find that she carries this characteristic to its logical extreme. Furthermore, we hear several times about the danger of catching the Roman fever, so when Daisy does become sick, we have been prepared for this by earlier allusions to the illness. In *The Turn of the Screw,* there is every type of indication that sooner or later the governess will confront the children with the presence of one of the apparitions. When she confronts Flora with the presence of Miss Jessel, the little girl becomes sick. As a result, we are prepared to accept the fact that Miles will die from his exposure to the apparition of Peter Quint. Thus, James uses foreshadowing to prepare the reader for the climactic events of the story.

QUESTIONS

DAISY MILLER

1. Why does James shift his setting from Switzerland to Italy?

2. What is the purpose of having a narrator who comes from America but has lived so long in Europe?

3. In addition to functioning as Winterborne's confidante, what other purpose does Mrs. Costello serve?

4. If Daisy's actions in going to the castle with Winterborne were innocent, why does he assume that her actions with Mr. Giovanelli are improper?

5. What is gained by having Daisy die at the end of the story?

6. Does Winterborne learn anything from his associations with Daisy?

7. Why does Mrs. Walker try to save Daisy and then later snub her?

8. What does Mr. Giovanelli expect from his relationship with Daisy?

9. Describe Daisy's system of values.

10. How innocent is Daisy of the fact that she is being improper?

THE TURN OF THE SCREW

1. What motivates the governess to accept such an unusual position?

2. Describe the circumstances surrounding each appearance of an apparition.

3. How does Mrs. Grose come to believe in the presence of the ghosts?

4 Why does James emphasize so strongly the sweetness and innocence of the children?

5. Why does the governess fail to investigate Miles' expulsion from school?

6. What is gained by having the governess relate the story?

7. How do you account for little Flora's illness at the end of the story?

8. What does the governess think of her employer?

9. Is it important that this was the governess' first position?

10. How responsible is the governess for the fate of the children?

SELECTED BIBLIOGRAPHY

Beach, J. W. *The Method of Henry James.* rev. ed. Philadelphia: Saifer, 1962.

Bewley, Marius. *The Complex Fate.* London: Chatto and Windus, 1952.

Dupee, F. W. (editor). *The Question of Henry James.* New York: Henry Holt and Company, 1945.

Edel, Leon. *The Modern Psychological Novel.* New York: Grove Press, 1959.

_____. *The Untried Years.* Philadelphia: Lippincott, 1962.

James, Henry. *Autobiography.* New York: Criterion Books, 1956.

Lubbock, Percy (editor). *The Letters of Henry James,* Two Volumes. New York: Charles Scribner's Sons, 1920.

McCarthy, Harold T. *Henry James: The Creative Process.* Toronto: A. S. Barnes and Co., 1955.

Matthiesen, F. O. and Murdock, Kenneth (editors). *The Notebooks of Henry James.* New York: Oxford University Press, 1947.

Matthiesen, F. O. and Murdock, Kenneth (editors). *The Major Phase.* London, New York: Oxford University Press, 1944.

NOTES

Your Guides to Successful Test Preparation.

Cliffs Test Preparation Guides
• *Complete* • *Concise* • *Functional* • *In-depth*

Efficient preparation means better test scores. Go with the experts and use *Cliffs Test Preparation Guides*. They focus on helping you know what to expect from each test, and their test-taking techniques have been proven in classroom programs nationwide. Recommended for individual use or as a part of a formal test preparation program.

Publisher's ISBN Prefix 0-8220

Qty.	ISBN	Title	Price	Qty.	ISBN	Title	Price
	2078-5	ACT	8.95		2044-0	Police Sergeant Exam	9.95
	2069-6	CBEST	8.95		2047-5	Police Officer Exam	14.95
	2056-4	CLAST	9.95		2049-1	Police Management Exam	17.95
	2071-8	ELM Review	8.95		2076-9	Praxis I: PPST	9.95
	2077-7	GED	11.95		2017-3	Praxis II: NTE Core Battery	14.95
	2061-0	GMAT	9.95		2074-2	SAT*	9.95
	2073-4	GRE	9.95		2325-3	SAT II*	14.95
	2066-1	LSAT	9.95		2072-6	TASP	8.95
	2046-7	MAT	12.95		2079-3	TOEFL w/cassettes	29.95
	2033-5	Math Review	8.95		2080-7	TOEFL Adv. Prac. (w/cass.)	24.95
	2048-3	MSAT	24.95		2034-3	Verbal Review	7.95
	2020-3	Memory Power for Exams	5.95		2043-2	Writing Proficiency Exam	8.95

Prices subject to change without notice.

Available at your booksellers, or send this form with your check or money order to **Cliffs Notes, Inc., P.O. Box 80728, Lincoln, NE 68501** http://www.cliffs.com

☐ Money order ☐ Check payable to Cliffs Notes, Inc.

☐ Visa ☐ Mastercard Signature_____

Card no. _____ Exp. date _____

Signature _____

Name _____

Address _____

City _____ State_____ Zip_____

*GRE, MSAT, Praxis PPST, NTE, TOEFL and Adv. Practice are registered trademarks of ETS. SAT is a registered trademark of CEEB.

Think Quick...Again

Now there are more Cliffs Quick Review® titles, providing help with more introductory level courses. Use Quick Reviews to increase your understanding of fundamental principles in a given subject, as well as to prepare for quizzes, midterms and finals.

Think quick with new Cliffs Quick Review titles. You'll find them at your bookstore or by returning the attached order form. Do better in the classroom, and on papers and tests with Cliffs Quick Reviews.